THE GREAT CFO'S

STORIES OF FINANCIAL LEADERSHIP

CA HASAN BASHA SHAIK

Made with ♥ on the Notion Press Platform
www.notionpress.com

This Book is Dedicated

To my dad ***"Shaik Gaffar Saab"***

For permission requests or any inquiries related to the use of the content in this book, and any services related to finance please feel free to contact on my email id is

Cahasanshaik@gmail.com

Contents

Foreword

The information provided in this book, "The Great CFOs: Stories of Financial Leadership," is intended for general informational purposes only. The stories, insights, and recommendations presented here are based on real-life and fictional scenarios to illustrate principles of financial leadership.

While every effort has been made to ensure the accuracy and relevance of the content, the field of finance is dynamic, and the specific circumstances of financial leadership may vary from one organisation to another. The book does not constitute professional financial, legal, or business advice. Readers are encouraged to seek the counsel of qualified professionals when making financial decisions or implementing financial strategies in their organisations.

The stories and examples included in this book are not endorsements of specific individuals or companies, and any resemblance to actual persons, living or dead, or real organisations is purely coincidental. The author and publisher disclaim any responsibility or liability for any potential inaccuracies or omissions in the content and for any consequences that may arise from the use of this information.

Readers are encouraged to exercise their discretion and judgement when applying the principles and strategies discussed in this book to their unique circumstances. The author and publisher do not assume any responsibility for the results or outcomes of such applications.

Acknowledgements

Conclusion

Summarise the key takeaways from the book.

Encourage readers to apply the insights and stories of successful CFOs in their own careers.

Appendix

Include additional resources, references, or tools to further assist readers in their journey to becoming great CFOs.

This outline provides a structure for a book on successful CFOs, narrated and written by CA Hasan Basha Shaik. It combines stories of financial leadership with expert commentary, making it a valuable resource for finance professionals and those aspiring to excel in their careers.

Prologue

The Great CFO's

Stories of Financial Leadership

Introduction

In the dynamic world of business, there exists a unique vocation of financial leadership, a role that transcends the boundaries of numbers and regulations. It's the realm of Chief Financial Officers (CFOs), individuals who steer the financial ship of organisations with unparalleled acumen, integrity, and strategic vision.

"The Great CFOs: Stories of Financial Leadership" is a tribute to these exceptional individuals (here from now onwards individual names referred as **The Great CFO's**) and a testament to their vital role in shaping the global economy. In the pages that follow, we embark on a journey through the financial landscapes of diverse industries, guided by the remarkable stories and experiences of those who have successfully navigated the complex world of corporate finance.

The role of a CFO extends far beyond the confines of balance sheets and quarterly reports. They are the stewards of fiscal responsibility, the architects of sound investment strategies, and the guardians of ethical financial conduct. In essence, they are the financial heartbeat of the organisations they serve, influencing decisions that impact employees, stakeholders, and society at large.

This book is not just a collection of stories; it is a testament to the power of financial leadership. As we explore the lives and careers of these Great CFOs, we uncover the qualities and skills that set them apart and discover the lessons they have to offer.

Through real-world case studies, personal insights, and the wealth of knowledge from the Great CFO's. We delve into the nuances of the CFO role. We learn how these individuals have tackled challenges, demonstrated unwavering integrity, and acted as strategic partners, driving their organisations toward financial success and sustainability.

Whether you are an aspiring financial leader, a seasoned CFO, or simply intrigued by the intricacies of financial stewardship, this book offers invaluable lessons. It is a testament to the importance of ethical leadership, the pursuit of knowledge, and the enduring significance of financial responsibility in a rapidly changing business environment.

As we embark on this journey, remember that behind every financial decision, every balance sheet, and every profit margin, there are exceptional individuals who have left an indelible mark on the world of finance. These are the Great CFOs, and this is their story.

Let us venture forth and uncover the essence of financial leadership together.

CHAPTER ONE

The CFO's Role in Modern Business

In the ever-evolving landscape of modern business, the Chief Financial Officer (CFO) holds a pivotal role, serving as the financial compass and strategic navigator of organisations. The complexity and dynamism of today's global markets demand that the CFO not only be well-versed in the intricacies of finance but also be an astute leader, visionary thinker, and ethical steward of corporate resources.

The Evolving Role of the CFO

Historically seen as the custodians of financial data and gatekeepers of fiscal regulations, CFOs have undergone a profound transformation in recent years. They have transitioned from number-crunching executives to key decision-makers, influencing the strategic direction of their organisations.

Modern CFOs are expected to:

1. Drive Financial Strategy: CFOs play a critical role in shaping the financial strategy of their organisations. They are instrumental in identifying growth opportunities, evaluating investments, and ensuring long-term financial sustainability.

2. Lead Risk Management: Managing financial risks has become a core responsibility of CFOs. They must assess, mitigate, and navigate risks in an increasingly volatile global economy.

3. Ensure Compliance and Transparency: With ever-changing regulatory landscapes, CFOs are responsible for ensuring compliance with financial reporting standards and maintaining transparency in financial operations.

4. Ethical Leadership: The expectation for ethical leadership has never been higher. CFOs are responsible for upholding the highest standards of integrity and ethical conduct, both internally and externally.

CFO as the Bridge between Finance and Strategy

A modern CFO is the bridge that connects the world of finance to the strategic objectives of an organisation. They collaborate closely with CEOs, boards of directors, and other key stakeholders to translate financial data into actionable strategies.

Through their financial expertise, CFOs provide valuable insights on:

- - Capital allocation and investment decisions
- - Cost optimization and efficiency
- - Identifying emerging market trends
- - Evaluating opportunities for mergers and acquisitions
- - Balancing short-term financial goals with long-term sustainability

Financial Stewardship and Sustainable Growth

A great CFO is not only concerned with the financial health of the organisation today but also with its long-term sustainability. They recognize that responsible financial management is not just about maximising profits in the short term but also about ensuring the organisation's ability to thrive for years to come.

In this chapter, we explore the dynamic and multifaceted role of the modern CFO. We will discover how they balance the demands of financial stewardship, risk management, and strategic leadership. Through the stories of Great CFOs and insights from Author CA Hasan Shaik, we'll delve deeper into the qualities and skills that empower these individuals to excel in their roles.

Join us on this journey as we explore the transformative journey of the CFO from traditional finance gatekeeper to a strategic partner in the business world.

CHAPTER TWO

QUALITIES THAT DEFINE GREAT CFOs

In the world of financial leadership, excellence is not solely determined by one's grasp of numbers or ability to analyse spreadsheets. While these skills are undeniably crucial, exceptional Chief Financial Officers (CFOs) possess a distinct set of qualities that set them apart as true luminaries in the field. These qualities extend beyond financial acumen and encompass the very essence of leadership, vision, and integrity.

The Essential Qualities of Great CFOs

1. Leadership: Great CFOs are not just financial experts; they are leaders who inspire and motivate their teams to achieve exceptional results. They possess the ability to steer an organisation through complex financial challenges with confidence and charisma.

2. Financial Acumen: Of course, a deep understanding of finance is a prerequisite for the role. Great CFOs not only comprehend the intricacies of financial data but also know how to leverage this knowledge to drive business success.

3. Strategic Thinking: These leaders think beyond the numbers. They have the vision to align financial strategy with the broader objectives of the organisation. They understand that the CFO's role is not limited to cost-cutting but extends to charting a path for sustainable growth.

4. Effective Communication: The ability to convey complex financial information in a clear and compelling manner is a hallmark of great CFOs. They bridge the gap between finance and non-finance professionals, fostering a collective understanding of financial goals and strategies.

5. Adaptability: In a rapidly changing business environment, adaptability is essential. Exceptional CFOs remain agile, continuously learning and adjusting their approaches to address new challenges and seize emerging opportunities.

Author CA Hasan Shaik's Insights:

1. Integrity as the Cornerstone: *"Integrity lies at the **heart of every great CFO.** It's about being steadfast in ethical conduct, even when faced with difficult decisions. This quality builds trust not only within the organisation but also with stakeholders and the wider financial community."*

2. Balancing Prudence and Risk-Taking: *"Great CFOs walk a fine line between prudence and calculated risk. They understand that avoiding risks altogether can be just as detrimental as taking reckless gambles. It's about making informed decisions that align with the organisation's risk appetite."*

3. Team Empowerment: *"A truly exceptional CFO understands that their success is intertwined with the success of their team. They empower their team members, providing them with opportunities for growth and development. This not only builds a stronger finance function but also contributes to* *the overall success of the organisation."*

4. Strategic Resource Allocation: *"Resource allocation is a critical aspect of financial leadership. Great CFOs have a knack for allocating resources in a way that maximises returns and aligns with the organisation's strategic priorities. They're adept at identifying areas where investments can yield the greatest impact."*

5. Continuous Learning and Innovation: *"The financial landscape is ever-evolving. Great CFOs have a hunger for knowledge and a willingness to embrace new technologies and methodologies. They stay ahead of industry trends and leverage innovation to drive efficiency and effectiveness in financial operations."*

6. Resilience in the Face of Adversity: *"The ability to maintain composure and make sound decisions during challenging times is a hallmark of a great CFO. They're not easily rattled by crises but rather, they step up as calm and decisive leaders, guiding their organisations through turbulence."*

7. Building Collaborative Relationships: *"Exceptional CFOs understand that they're not isolated figures in the organisation. They actively build relationships with other departments, the CEO, the board, and external stakeholders. This collaborative approach ensures that financial strategies are aligned with broader organisational goals."*

8. Long-term Vision and Sustainability: *"While managing day-to-day financial operations is crucial, great CFOs keep an eye on the long game. They're dedicated to building financial foundations that support sustainable growth and resilience over the years, rather than pursuing short-term gains."*

These insights from CA Hasan Basha Shaik provide a deeper understanding of the qualities that define great CFOs, emphasizing the importance of integrity, strategic thinking, team empowerment, and adaptability. They offer valuable guidance for aspiring financial leaders and serve as a source of inspiration for current CFOs looking to elevate their roles.

CHAPTER THREE

SUCCESSFUL CFOs IN ACTION

The qualities that define great CFOs are not static traits but dynamic forces that come to life when put into action. In this chapter, we embark on a journey to witness these exceptional qualities in motion through the inspiring stories of successful Chief Financial Officers (CFOs). These individuals, through their wisdom, courage, and unwavering dedication, have made an indelible mark on the world of finance.

The Stories of Financial Pioneers

Through the narratives that follow, we delve into the lives and careers of CFOs who have demonstrated extraordinary leadership, financial acumen, strategic thinking, and more. These luminaries have proven that these qualities are not mere concepts but powerful instruments that can transform organisations and industries.

The Visionary Transformer: Meet The Great CFO, a CFO who, through strategic thinking and adept financial management, spearheaded a complete turnaround of a struggling manufacturing company. His story unveils how a great CFO can reshape the destiny of an organisation.

The Ethical Champion: Explore the life of The Great CFO, whose unyielding commitment to ethical leadership led to the creation of robust corporate governance and a culture of integrity. The Great CFO journey is a testament to how great CFOs are the ethical compasses of the financial world.

The Global Strategist: Journey with The Great CFO as he navigates the complexities of international finance, leveraging his financial acumen to guide his company's global expansion. His story is a compelling example of how great CFOs master the intricacies of a diverse and ever-changing world market.

The Communicator: Discover the profound impact of The Great CFO, a CFO renowned for his ability to communicate complex financial data in a way that inspires and unites diverse teams. His story underscores the pivotal role great CFOs play in bridging the gap between finance and other departments.

Insights from CA Hasan Basha Shaik

Through the lens of Author CA Hasan Basha Shaik, a revered expert in the field, we gain deeper insights into these real-world accounts of financial leadership. His reflections illuminate how these exceptional qualities materialised into remarkable achievements.

As we journey through the experiences of these successful CFOs, we find lessons that extend beyond finance. These stories reveal that while financial prowess is essential, the qualities that define great CFOs, when harnessed and applied, have the power to drive innovation, transformation, and profound positive change.

Join us as we walk alongside these financial pioneers, learning from their journeys and absorbing the wisdom they've gained through their extraordinary careers. Together, we will witness the qualities of great CFOs come to life and realise their potential to impact the financial world and beyond.

CHAPTER FOUR

Overcoming Challenges And Navigating Complexities

The path to greatness is often lined with obstacles and intricacies that require more than just financial acumen. It demands resilience, creativity, and an unwavering commitment to the values and principles that define a true financial leader. In this chapter, we delve into the challenges that Chief Financial Officers (CFOs) encounter and how they navigate these complexities with grace and expertise.

The Complex Financial Landscape

In today's business environment, CFOs are confronted with a myriad of complex financial challenges, from volatile markets and economic uncertainties to evolving regulatory requirements. It is the ability to confront and overcome these challenges that truly separates exceptional CFOs from the rest.

- Economic Turbulence: We explore how The Great CFO steered his organisation through a period of economic recession, demonstrating his capacity to make tough financial decisions while safeguarding long-term sustainability.

In 2020, The Great CFO, the CFO of a big manufacturing company, faced a major problem when the COVID-19 pandemic caused a sudden economic downturn. The company, which was doing well before, had to deal with a sharp drop in business, supply chain issues, and financial market uncertainty. The Great CFO key actions included managing cash carefully, testing the company's financial health under different scenarios, cutting costs while protecting jobs, and negotiating with lenders for better financial terms. The Great CFOalso kept an eye on the company's long-term strategy and communicated openly with the team. His strong leadership and smart decisions helped the company survive the tough times, and when the economy started to recover, the company was in a better position to grow. This case shows how a CFO's strategic thinking and financial expertise can make a big difference during challenging economic situations.

- Regulatory Evolution: The story of The Great CFO, highlighting his role in ensuring compliance and transparency in the face of ever-changing financial regulations. We see how his adaptability and understanding of compliance complexities have been crucial.

In this case study, we meet The Great CFO, a CFO at a financial company dealing with changing rules about keeping customer information safe. He led his team through a complex web of new regulations. The Great CFO made important decisions like investing in high-tech security and training the team. He talked a lot with regulators and other experts to make sure the company followed the new rules. Through these efforts, the company not only met the regulations but also became known for keeping customer data safe. This case shows how a CFO's leadership and smart decisions can help a company adapt and succeed in a changing regulatory world.

- ***Risk Management Mastery:*** Join us in uncovering how The Great CFO, a Master of Risk Management, skilfully navigated the intricacies of financial risk, helping his company thrive in an unpredictable world.

- ***Resilience and Creative Solutions*** Great CFOs do not merely confront challenges; they transform them into opportunities for growth and innovation. These financial leaders understand that complexity demands creative thinking and an unwavering commitment to the ethical principles that guide their actions.

- ***Innovative Financing***: We explore how The Great CFO, faced with limited resources, creatively structured financial solutions that enabled his company's ambitious expansion.

In this short story, we meet The Great CFO, the CFO of a tech startup facing a lack of funds to grow. The Great CFO had to be creative to find solutions. He started a campaign to get regular people to invest in the company, formed partnerships with other businesses to save money, and used unique financing methods. The Great CFO also made sure the company spent money wisely and introduced new ways to make money. His creative thinking not only helped the startup survive but also made it thrive and grow in a competitive market. This story shows how a CFO's creative solutions can solve financial challenges and lead a company to success.

- ***Ethical Dilemmas:*** Follow The Great CFO journey as he encounters an ethical dilemma that challenges the very core of his principles. His story demonstrates the unwavering commitment of great CFOs to ethical leadership.

Insights from CA Hasan Basha Shaik

Author CA Hasan lends his wisdom to the stories of overcoming challenges and navigating complexities. Drawing from his extensive experience, he shares insights into the strategies and approaches that these exceptional CFOs used to tackle complex financial landscapes.

These real-world accounts serve as a testament to the resourcefulness, innovation, and resilience of great CFOs. As we journey through the trials and triumphs of these financial leaders, we are reminded that while challenges may be inevitable, their impact can be transformed through exceptional leadership.

Innovative financing *refers to creative methods and approaches to raise funds or manage financial resources. Here are some examples of innovative financing:*

1. ***Crowdfunding:*** *Platforms like Kickstarter and Indiegogo allow individuals to contribute small amounts of money to fund projects, products, or startups.*

2. ***Peer-to-Peer (P2P) Lending:*** *P2P lending platforms connect individuals or businesses seeking loans with potential lenders, often at competitive interest rates.*

3. ***Social Impact Bonds:*** *These bonds provide funding for social programs or initiatives with the promise of financial returns based on predefined social outcomes.*

4. ***Revenue-Based Financing:*** *Companies can secure funds based on projected revenue, paying investors a percentage of their revenue until a certain cap or return is reached.*

5. ***Venture Debt:*** *A hybrid financing option for startups, combining elements of debt and equity, often offered by venture debt firms.*

*6. **Angel Investors and Venture Capital:** While not new, these traditional financing methods continue to evolve, with venture capital firms and angel investors seeking innovative startups to fund.*

*7. **Green Bonds:** These bonds fund environmentally friendly projects and initiatives, attracting investors interested in sustainability.*

*8. **Cryptocurrency and Initial Coin Offerings (ICOs):** Companies can raise funds through the sale of digital tokens or coins, appealing to investors in the cryptocurrency space.*

*9. **Microfinance:** This involves providing small loans to individuals, often in developing countries, to help them start or expand small businesses.*

*10. **Strategic Partnerships and Alliances:** Companies can collaborate with other businesses to share resources, reduce costs, and access new markets.*

*11. **Equipment Financing:** Businesses can lease or finance equipment rather than purchasing it outright, preserving capital for other uses.*

*12. **Factoring:** Companies can sell their accounts receivable at a discount to receive immediate cash, improving cash flow.*

*13. **Subscription-Based Models:** Transitioning to subscription-based services can provide a steady stream of recurring revenue for businesses.*

*14. **Inventory Financing:** Companies can secure financing based on the value of their inventory, freeing up capital that would otherwise be tied up.*

*15. **Securitization:** Financial institutions can bundle loans or assets into securities that can be sold to investors, freeing up capital for further lending.*

These examples illustrate the diverse range of innovative financing methods that businesses and individuals can employ to address their financial needs, whether it's raising capital for a startup, funding a specific project, or managing financial resources efficiently.

Join us in this chapter to explore the resilience, creativity, and unwavering commitment to ethical financial conduct that allow CFOs to overcome complexities and emerge as financial champions.

CHAPTER FIVE

The Role of Ethics and Integrity

In the realm of financial leadership, the importance of ethics and unwavering integrity cannot be overstated. Exceptional Chief Financial Officers (CFOs) not only excel in managing numbers and navigating complexities but also stand as ethical compasses in the world of finance. In this chapter, we explore the pivotal role of ethics and integrity in the lives and careers of these financial leaders.

- The Bedrock of Ethical Leadership

Ethics and integrity are the bedrock upon which financial leadership is built. Exceptional CFOs understand that their actions impact not only their organisations but also the broader financial community and society as a whole. They are committed to upholding the highest standards of ethical conduct.

- A Legacy of Integrity: The story of The Great CFO, who, throughout his career, maintained an unblemished record of ethical financial leadership. His journey reveals the far-reaching impact of ethical conduct in the financial world.

In the world of finance, integrity is a timeless and invaluable trait, and it's exemplified in the story of The Great CFO, a seasoned CFO with a legacy of integrity. Throughout his career, The Great CFO always made principled decisions, even when faced with tempting shortcuts. His unwavering commitment to financial ethics not only earned him trust within his organisation but also made him a respected figure in the financial industry. The Great CFO legacy serves as a testament to the enduring importance of integrity in financial leadership, showing that, in the long run, doing what's right is always the best financial decision.

- **Navigating Ethical Crossroads**: Join us as the Great CFO encounters an ethical dilemma that puts his principles to the test. His story exemplifies the unwavering commitment of great CFOs to ethical leadership.

- Upholding Transparency and Trust

CFOs are not just stewards of financial resources but also guardians of transparency and trust. They are responsible for ensuring that financial operations are conducted with integrity, accountability, and transparency.

- **The Transparency Advocate:** In the narrative of The Great CFO, we discover how he championed transparency in financial reporting, inspiring a culture of openness and trust within his organisation.

- **Safeguarding Stakeholder Interests**: We follow The Great CFO journey as he demonstrates the ethical duty of CFOs to safeguard the interests of shareholders, employees, and the public through transparent financial practices.

Insights from CA Hasan Basha Shaik

Author CA Hasan Shaik provides profound insights into the importance of ethics and integrity in the world of finance. Drawing from his expertise, he sheds light on the ethical principles that underpin the stories of the exceptional CFOs featured in this chapter.

As we explore the narratives of ethical champions in the financial world, we are reminded that success in financial leadership is not measured solely by numbers but also by the trust and confidence that a CFO inspires. Join us in this chapter to witness the profound impact of ethics and integrity and the enduring legacy of financial leaders who uphold these principles.

CHAPTER SIX

Navigating Financial Reporting and Regulatory Compliance

In the intricate web of finance, financial reporting and regulatory compliance stand as formidable challenges. Exceptional Chief Financial Officers (CFOs) possess the knowledge and expertise to not only interpret financial data but also ensure that their organisations meet the ever-evolving regulatory standards. In this chapter, we embark on a journey to explore how great CFOs navigate the complexities of financial reporting and compliance with precision and integrity.

- The Balancing Act of Financial Reporting

Financial reporting is the backbone of transparency in the financial world. It is a language of numbers that great CFOs master to communicate the health and performance of their organisations to stakeholders, regulators, and the public.

- **The Reporting Maestro:** Discover the story of The Great CFO, a CFO renowned for his mastery of financial reporting. Through his journey, we witness how exceptional CFOs balance the art of clarity and precision in financial communication.

- **The Quarterly Challenge:** Follow The Great CFO as he successfully leads his organisation through the demanding process of quarterly financial reporting, ensuring compliance with stringent regulations while presenting a clear financial narrative.

- Regulatory Evolution and Compliance

The regulatory landscape in finance is a constantly shifting terrain. Great CFOs not only keep pace with these changes but also lead their organisations in adapting to the evolving standards.

- **Championing Compliance:** Join us in the narrative of The Great CFO, a CFO dedicated to maintaining a culture of compliance. His story illustrates the critical role of great CFOs in ensuring that organisations adhere to rigorous regulatory requirements.

- **Navigating Regulatory Challenges**: We explore the journey of The Great CFO, who adeptly navigated his organisation through a complex regulatory challenge, demonstrating the strategic acumen required to address compliance issues.

Insights from CA Hasan Basha Shaik

Author CA Hasan Shaik shares invaluable insights into the world of financial reporting and regulatory compliance. Drawing from his extensive knowledge, he provides a deeper understanding of the strategies and approaches that great CFOs use to address these complexities.

As we journey through the narratives of financial reporting and compliance, we gain an appreciation for the meticulous nature of these tasks and the critical role great CFOs play in maintaining transparency and accountability in the financial world. Join us in this chapter to uncover the precision, dedication, and unwavering commitment to regulatory compliance that define financial leadership at its best.

CHAPTER SEVEN

Building Successful Finance Teams

The journey of The Great CFO is not one taken alone. Exceptional CFOs understand the importance of surrounding themselves with talented finance teams to achieve their organisation's financial objectives. In this chapter, we explore how great CFOs build and lead successful finance teams, fostering a culture of excellence and collaboration.

- The Architect of Finance Teams

CFOs are not just financial strategists; they are also architects of the teams that execute these strategies. They recognize the importance of assembling the right talents, developing their skills, and aligning their efforts with the financial vision.

- The Talent Developer

Join us in discovering the story of The Great CFO, a CFO who excels in identifying and nurturing finance talents within his organisation. His journey highlights the pivotal role of great CFOs in developing future financial leaders.

- **Fostering Collaboration**: Explore the experiences of The Great CFO as he skillfully creates a culture of collaboration within his finance team, where each member contributes their unique expertise to achieve common financial goals.

- Effective Leadership and Motivation

The Great CFO not only selects the best talents but also inspires and motivates their teams to achieve financial excellence. They lead by example, setting the standards for ethical conduct and financial expertise.

- **Ethical Leadership**: We learn from the experiences of The Great CFO, who places unwavering emphasis on ethical conduct within his finance team. His story demonstrates the enduring impact of ethics in leadership.

- **Inspiring Excellence**: Follow the journey of The Great CFO as he inspires his finance team to consistently deliver exceptional results. His story illustrates how great CFOs set high standards for performance and achievement.

Insights from CA Hasan Basha Shaik

Author CA Hasan shares his insights into the art of building and leading successful finance teams. Drawing from his vast expertise, he provides valuable guidance on the qualities and strategies that great CFOs employ to develop high-performing teams.

As we explore the narratives of building successful finance teams, we discover the critical role that CFOs play in nurturing financial talents, fostering collaboration, and inspiring excellence. Join us in this chapter to witness the powerful impact of great CFOs not only in managing numbers but also in cultivating a culture of financial excellence within their organisations

CHAPTER EIGHT

THE CFO AS A STRATEGIC PARTNER

In the modern business landscape, the Chief Financial Officer (CFO) is no longer confined to the role of a financial gatekeeper. Exceptional CFOs have evolved into strategic partners who work hand in hand with CEOs and boards of directors to shape the future of their organisations. In this chapter, we explore how great CFOs have embraced this strategic role, becoming catalysts for innovation and growth.

- ***Shaping Organisational Strategy***

The Great CFO's are not passive observers of corporate strategy but active architects. They leverage their financial acumen to identify growth opportunities, drive innovation, and align financial strategies with broader organisational objectives.

- ***The Strategic Visionary***: Discover the story of The Great CFO, a CFO who played a pivotal role in reshaping his organisation's strategic direction. His journey unveils the transformational power of great CFOs as strategic partners.

- ***Innovation Catalyst***: Join us in exploring the experiences of The Great CFO, who spearheaded financial innovations that not only increased efficiency but also positioned his organisation at the forefront of industry trends.

Balancing Risk and Reward

The strategic CFO understands that innovation and growth are inherently tied to risk. They master the art of balancing risk and reward, ensuring that financial strategies are not only ambitious but also sustainable.

- ***Risk Management Expert***: Learn from the journey of The Great CFO, a CFO who excelled in managing financial risks and enabling his organisation to navigate complex economic landscapes with confidence.

- ***Strategic Risk-Taker***: Follow the story of The Great CFO as he takes calculated risks to drive his organisation's growth. His narrative illustrates how great CFOs play a pivotal role in guiding their organisations through strategic challenges.

Insights from CA Hasan Basha Shaik

Author CA Hasan Shaik shares his insights into the strategic aspect of the CFO's role, offering guidance on how CFOs can become effective partners in shaping organisational strategy. His perspective enriches the understanding of the strategies and qualities that define great CFOs in this role.

As we journey through the narratives of strategic partnerships, we witness the transformative influence of great CFOs in shaping the destiny of their organisations. Join us in this chapter to explore the strategic vision, innovation, and risk management that define the CFO as a strategic partner, driving their organisations towards success.

CHAPTER NINE

THE GLOBAL CFO

In our interconnected world, the role of a Chief Financial Officer (CFO) extends beyond national borders. Exceptional CFOs are not just financial leaders within their organisations but also global strategists who navigate the complexities of international finance and contribute to the success of their companies on a global scale. In this chapter, we explore the dynamic and challenging role of the global CFO.

- Navigating International Finance

The global CFO operates in a diverse and ever-changing international financial landscape. They must understand international markets, currency fluctuations, and geopolitical factors to make informed decisions that drive their organisations' global success.

- Mastering Currency Markets

Discover the journey of The Great CFO, a global CFO who adeptly managed currency risk and optimised foreign exchange operations to safeguard his company's international profits.

- Global Market Expansion

Join us as The Great CFO Turner charts the course for his organisation's global expansion. His narrative showcases how great CFOs leverage their financial acumen to seize opportunities on the global stage.

- **Cultural Intelligence and Collaboration**

In addition to financial expertise, global CFOs must possess cultural intelligence and the ability to collaborate with teams from diverse backgrounds. These qualities are essential for building successful international partnerships and navigating cultural nuances.

- **Cultural Bridge-Builder**: Explore the story of The Great CFO, a CFO who excelled in building bridges with international partners and understanding the cultural dynamics of global markets.

- **International Collaboration**: Witness how The Great CFO ability to collaborate effectively with international teams allowed his organisation to thrive in a competitive global landscape.

Insights from CA Hasan Basha Shaik

Author CA Hasan Basha Shaik provides insights into the unique challenges and opportunities that global CFOs face. His expertise sheds light on the strategies and qualities that make CFOs effective global financial leaders.

As we explore the narratives of global CFOs, we gain an appreciation for the intricacies of international finance and the qualities that allow these financial leaders to excel on a global scale. Join us in this chapter to discover the global mindset, currency mastery, cultural intelligence, and international collaboration that define the role of the global CFO

CHAPTER TEN

Crisis Management and Resilience

In the tumultuous world of business, crises are an inevitable reality. Exceptional Chief Financial Officers (CFOs) not only excel in times of stability but also demonstrate their mettle in the face of adversity. In this chapter, we explore the role of great CFOs in crisis management and how their resilience and leadership skills shine during challenging times.

- The CFO in Crisis

When a crisis strikes, the CFO is often on the front lines, managing financial impacts, making tough decisions, and providing steady guidance. Exceptional CFOs are resilient leaders who maintain their composure and drive their organisations through turbulent waters.

- **Financial Crisis Navigator:** Meet The Great CFOr, a CFO who played a crucial role in steering his organisation through a financial crisis. His story illustrates the indispensable role of great CFOs in crisis management.

- **Pandemic Response Leader**: Join us as The Great CFO demonstrates his leadership during a global pandemic, showcasing the adaptability and strategic thinking that great CFOs bring to crisis management.

- **Balancing Short-term and Long-term Resilience**

The Great CFO understands that crisis management is not just about surviving the moment but also ensuring long-term resilience. They balance short-term financial stability with strategies that will lead their organisations to thrive in the aftermath of crisis.

- **Sustainable Recovery Planner**: Witness the journey of The Great CFO as he develops a sustainable recovery plan that not only helps his organisation rebound from a crisis but also positions it for long-term success.

- **Ethical Crisis Management**: Explore how The Great CFO handled an ethical crisis, preserving his organisation's reputation and integrity through unwavering ethical leadership.

Insights from CA Hasan Basha Shaik

Author CA Hasan Shaik offers insights into the unique challenges of crisis management and the qualities that great CFOs possess to navigate and lead during difficult times. His expertise provides a deeper understanding of the strategies and resilience that define CFOs in crisis.

As we delve into the narratives of crisis management and resilience, we discover the indispensable role of great CFOs in guiding their organisations through adversity. Join us in this chapter to explore the leadership, resilience, and adaptability that great CFOs bring to crisis situations and learn from their experiences in turbulent times.

CHAPTER ELEVEN

PERSONAL AND PROFESSIONAL GROWTH

In the ever-evolving world of financial leadership, the journey to excellence extends beyond mastering spreadsheets and budgets. It's a path of personal and professional growth, where exceptional CFOs not only excel in their roles but also continuously evolve, both as individuals and leaders. In this chapter, we embark on a transformative exploration of self-improvement and its profound impact on the financial landscape.

The CFO's Path to Growth:

The journey of personal and professional growth commences with self-awareness. Exceptional CFOs recognize the power of understanding themselves—their strengths, weaknesses, and growth opportunities. They actively seek feedback, embrace self-reflection, and use this foundation to elevate their leadership.

Balancing Technical Proficiency with Soft Skills:

While technical prowess remains essential in finance, great CFOs appreciate the significance of soft skills. They refine their communication, leadership, and interpersonal abilities, realizing that the capacity to collaborate and inspire is as influential as financial acumen.

A Commitment to Lifelong Learning:

In a rapidly changing financial landscape, the best CFOs are lifelong learners. They remain current with industry trends, emerging technologies, and regulatory shifts. Whether through formal education or perpetual self-study, they stay dedicated to the art of financial mastery.

The Power of Networking and Mentorship:

Great CFOs understand the value of forging networks and embracing mentorship. They cultivate connections with peers, industry luminaries, and mentors who offer invaluable guidance and unwavering support throughout their profession.

Building Resilience and Adaptability:

In a world marked by economic volatility and business uncertainties, personal and professional growth involves the cultivation of resilience. Exceptional CFOs exhibit the ability to adapt to change, navigate crises, and emerge from challenges even more resilient.

Ethical Leadership as a Guiding Light:

Personal growth goes hand in hand with ethical leadership. Great CFOs consistently uphold the highest ethical standards, setting an unwavering example for their teams and organisations. They recognize that trust and integrity are the foundational stones of enduring success.

Contributing Beyond the Balance Sheet:

Personal growth transcends the confines of the boardroom. Great CFOs often engage in community service and philanthropic ventures, comprehending the profound impact they can make outside their professional spheres.

Insights from CA Hasan Basha Shaik

Author CA Hasan Shaik offers insights Personal and professional growth is a ceaseless journey for The Great CFOs. It's a commitment to self-improvement, ethical leadership, and lifelong education. In this chapter, we delve into the experiences and wisdom of CFOs who have embraced growth not only as a professional necessity but also as a personal aspiration. Their stories and insights illuminate the path for those aspiring to become exceptional CFOs, emphasising that financial leadership isn't just about managing numbers; it's about growing as leaders and as individuals.

CHAPTER TWELVE

THE FUTURE OF FINANCIAL LEADERSHIP

As we journey through the stories and insights of great CFOs, we also cast our gaze forward, contemplating the exciting and ever-changing landscape of financial leadership. In this final chapter, we explore the emerging trends, challenges, and opportunities that will shape the role of the CFO in the future.

The Digital Revolution and Data-Driven Finance:

The future of financial leadership is undeniably digital. CFOs will increasingly harness the power of data analytics, artificial intelligence, and automation to drive strategic decision-making. The ability to extract valuable insights from data will be a defining skill for the CFO of tomorrow.

Sustainability and ESG:

Environmental, Social, and Governance (ESG) factors will play a prominent role in financial leadership. CFOs will be at the forefront of integrating ESG principles into financial strategies, demonstrating that sustainability is not only good for the planet but also for the bottom line.

Cybersecurity and Risk Management:

As businesses rely more on digital infrastructure, CFOs will need to be vigilant in cybersecurity. Managing financial risks associated with data breaches and cyber threats will be a paramount concern, requiring a blend of financial acumen and technological awareness.

Globalization and Geopolitical Factors:

The world continues to shrink as globalization advances. CFOs will navigate complex international financial landscapes, considering the impact of geopolitical factors, trade policies, and global economic trends on their organizations.

Ethical Finance and Governance:

The call for ethical finance and transparent governance will persist. CFOs will be instrumental in ensuring their organizations adhere to the highest ethical standards,

recognizing that integrity is not just a choice but an imperative for long-term success.

Agility and Adaptability:

The future CFO will be agile and adaptable. The ability to respond swiftly to changing market dynamics, economic shifts, and unforeseen challenges will be a defining characteristic of financial leadership.

Inclusive Leadership:

CFOs will recognize the importance of inclusive leadership, valuing diversity and fostering inclusive workplace cultures. Inclusion will not only be a moral obligation but also a source of innovation and competitiveness.

Insights from CA Hasan Basha Shaik

Author CA Hasan Shaik provides insights the future of financial leadership is a realm of infinite possibilities and challenges. In this closing chapter, we glimpse into the horizon of finance and gain insights into the ever-evolving role of the CFO. The great CFOs of tomorrow will be agile, data-driven, ethically conscious, and inclusive leaders who drive their organisations toward a sustainable and prosperous future.

As we conclude our exploration of financial leadership, we are reminded that the journey is ongoing. The legacy of great CFOs is not just in the stories we've uncovered but in the future they inspire, the leadership they embody, and the enduring impact they leave on the financial world.

Conclusion

In the pages of this book, we've embarked on a journey through the dynamic and multifaceted world of Chief Financial Officers (CFOs). These exceptional financial leaders have demonstrated not only a profound understanding of financial principles but also a unique set of qualities and skills that set them apart in the world of financial leadership.

From their roles as strategic partners, global visionaries, and ethical compasses to their exceptional abilities in managing crises, great CFOs have showcased the diverse dimensions of their roles. They have led organisations through stability and adversity, always with an unwavering commitment to the highest standards of ethical conduct and the future growth and success of their organisations.

The stories and insights shared in this book serve as a testament to the enduring impact that great CFOs make on the financial world and the broader business community. They inspire us not only with their financial acumen but also with their leadership, resilience, and vision.

As we conclude this journey, let us carry forward the lessons and inspiration gained from these remarkable individuals. The world of financial leadership continues to evolve, and the principles and qualities exemplified by great CFOs remain a guiding light for the future.

Appendix: Additional Resources

In this appendix, we provide a list of additional resources that can further enrich your understanding of financial leadership, the role of CFOs, and related topics. These resources include books, articles, websites, and organisations that delve deeper into the subject matter discussed in this book. We encourage you to explore these materials to expand your knowledge and insights.

Books:

1. "The Lean CFO: Architect of the Lean Management System" by Nicholas S. Katko

2. "CFO Techniques: A Hands-On Guide to Keeping Your Business Solvent and Successful" by Marina Guerrero and Rafael Matos

3. "CFO Fundamentals: Your Quick Guide to Internal Controls, Financial Reporting, IFRS, Web 2.0, Cloud Computing, and More" by Jae K. Shim and Joel G. Siegel

Websites:

1. The Wall Street Journal CFO Journal: www.wsj.com/cfo

2. Harvard Business Review CFO Section: hbr.org/cfo

3. Financial Executives International: [www.financialexecutives.org]
(https://www.financialexecutives.org)

Organisations:

1. Institute of Chartered Accountants of India (ICAI): www.icai.org

2. Institute of Cost & Management Accountants of India (ICMAI): [www.icmai.org]

3. The CFO Leadership Council: cfolc.com

Articles:

1. "The Evolving Role of the CFO" - Harvard Business Review

2. "Ethical Leadership and the Role of the CFO" - Forbes

3. "The Strategic CFO: Creating Value in a Dynamic Market" - Deloitte Insights

www.ingramcontent.com/pod-product-compliance
Lightning Source LLC
La Vergne TN
LVHW091238150826
845673LV00003B/1198

* 9 7 9 8 8 9 1 8 6 1 1 1 4 *